Become an Outstanding Manager

Become an Outstanding Manager

Fourteen Great Principles

Edward Schmidt

Copyright © 2016 Edward Schmidt
All rights reserved.
ISBN-13: 9781537096469
ISBN-10: 153709646X
Library of Congress Control Number: 2016915102
CreateSpace Independent Publishing Platform
North Charleston, South Carolina

About Edward Schmidt

Edward Schmidt worked as a midlevel manager for sixteen years in the New York State Department of Transportation (NYSDOT). He managed the successful development of its first electronic consultant-selection system (which is still in operation). Since consultants perform about half the department's designs of highways and bridges, this was an important and high-profile project.

After presenting the new system at a conference attended by over three hundred consultants, Ed accepted a position managing the two groups tasked with the responsibility of overseeing the department's consultant-hiring practices.

Ed was respected by the many managers and staff who dealt with him. He enjoyed helping people—and the organization overall—become more successful. Ed wrote this book to help managers who are looking for a better approach to management. He hopes this book will help them achieve a richer and more productive career in management.

This book is dedicated to my mother and father, who encouraged me with patience and kindness through the many changes in my life; to my two brothers, Ron and Ken, who have also been there for me; and to three people who always cheer me on—my wonderful wife, Jayne; my son, Paul; and my daughter, Karen.

Acknowledgments

I thank my coworkers and friends for encouraging me to write this book. In particular, I thank William Dollison for his help in editing the book and encouraging me to keep going. I hope that it helps managers find a different way to approach management—a way that will improve their performance and lives and the lives of their staff, other managers, and anyone else they deal with in their work.

Contents

About Edward Schmidt · v
Acknowledgments · ix
Preface: Why You Should Read This Book · · · · · · · · · · · · xiii
Introduction: My Management Background · · · · · · · · · · · xv

Principle 1	A Manager Should Be a Servant Leader · · · · · · · · · · · · · · · · ·	1
Principle 2	Life Is More Important than Work · · · · · · · · · · · · · · · · · · ·	4
Principle 3	Always Try to Be Positive ·	7
Principle 4	Want What Is Best for Employees · · · · · · · · · · · · · · · · · · ·	11
Principle 5	Listen to Your Staff ·	13
Principle 6	Respect All Employees and Treat Them Equally · · · · · · · ·	14
Principle 7	Always Make Time for Your Staff · · · · · · · · · · · · · · · · · ·	15
Principle 8	Encourage Employees to Bring Forth New Ideas · · · · · · · ·	17
Principle 9	Promote Teamwork and Organizational Goals · · · · · · · · · ·	18
Principle 10	Empower Employees by Thoroughly Training Them · · · · ·	20
Principle 11	About Performance Evaluations ·	22
Principle 12	Continually Look at the Process for Opportunities to Simplify ·	24
Principle 13	Be Patient, Thick Skinned, and Long Suffering · · · · · · · · ·	26
Principle 14	Help Your Managers Succeed ·	28

Examples of How to Apply These Principles in
Real-Life Situations ·31
As a Manager, How Am I Doing? A Brief Checklist · · · · · · ·33
Conclusion· ·37
About the Author· ·39

Preface: Why You Should Read This Book

Are you looking for a better way to manage? If you are, then the principles laid out here may be what you are looking for. They can revolutionize your view of what a manager's role is and how managers should function.

This book presents an approach to management that creates a more positive, motivating, and productive atmosphere for you, your staff, and others in the organization. It contains a concise description of the fourteen principles that define this approach. It certainly does not contain everything you need to know about management. But even so, applying these principles will help you become a better manager—even an outstanding one.

I am sharing these principles to help others enjoy a better and more productive life as managers. I spent my life in the public sector, where it was difficult to reward employees—financially or otherwise. Whether you are working in the public sector as I did or in the private sector, I believe these principles can be successfully applied. Some friends in the private sector have also found my principles useful.

I discussed my principles with many employees both within the agency where I worked and people who worked elsewhere. They are the people we are trying to manage in a better way, and we should listen to them. The feedback I received was very positive. If you have doubts about this approach, go ahead and speak with people about these principles and see if they appreciate the management method that is laid out here.

I would not be surprised if many managers took strong issue with my approach. I don't wish to debate these ideas with those who prefer to stick to their own methods. But if you are open minded, then I encourage you to read this book.

I know managers may be suspicious of yet another management book. I also know how busy you can be and how limited your time is. However, this is not a long discussion of procedures. It is not a theoretical work on doing your job, nor is it a book that is based on a survey of other managers. This is based on my real-life experiences. I have tried to make this short, practical, easy to read, and easy to reference.

I am confident that if you ask workers what they do not like about management and share some of my ideas with them, you will find their responses will validate what I am saying in this book.

Introduction: My Management Background

My last position was where I ultimately came to the management approach I describe in this book. I suspect that those people who worked with me when I first became a manager would be surprised at how I manage today.

I started with the New York State Department of Transportation as a junior engineer. I worked as a state inspector on highway- and bridge-construction projects until 1976. I then accepted a senior civil-engineer position in the main office. As I received promotions, I realized I eventually wanted to move into middle management. I read books on management and attended every training opportunity I could to become a better manager.

About twenty years after starting to work with the state, I was promoted to a middle-management position in the office that managed consultants designing highways and bridges for New York—the Contract Management Bureau. I worked there for nine years, first developing a new consultant-selection process and then managing the two sections that conducted the consultant-selection process. There, I was privileged to work with a bureau director whose example and advice helped to finalize my approach to management.

When I was in the process of retiring after thirty-seven years, I was surprised by and deeply grateful for the compliments I received from various members of my staff. They said such things as these:

"You made coming to work fun."

"You are the best manager I ever worked for."

"Your staff would do anything for you."

I believe my approach made it enjoyable to work with people, even difficult people; it helped me work with people to make them be the best they could be; it helped me function with other managers in a way that supported them; it helped me develop employees who would sacrifice for organizational goals; it helped increase morale, reward employees, and develop teamwork.

I thought maybe my management philosophy might help other managers.

Principle 1

A Manager Should Be a Servant Leader

Just as Jesus said (from a spiritual perspective) that to be great means to be the servant of all, managers must essentially be servants to their staffs, their own managers, and the other managers at their level. Helping others succeed is your job.

Just as Jesus was concerned about having compassion for the people around him, so should managers have compassion toward the people with whom they work.

These two elements of being a servant manager—being a servant and being compassionate—work together. As you help others succeed, you are also concerned about them and see them as human beings.

One employee I spoke with said one of the biggest things wrong with managers where she worked was that they did not care about her as a person—they had absolutely no interest in what was going on in the personal lives of their staff members. They never asked about her life and never supported her efforts to improve herself. (She was currently pursuing a postgraduate degree.)

Following principle one instead brings forth workers willing to go out of their way to help you meet your organizational goals. It makes your job more rewarding and productive, and it will help make the jobs of those around you more rewarding and productive.

Let me be clear—being a servant does not mean you are a weak leader. It does not mean you are not "in charge." Of course I had the last say at meetings I conducted with my staff, and of course I expressed differences with managers above me. But my approach to dealing with others was based on the belief that contributing to the success of those around me was the best way to advance the organization's goals.

I saw myself as essentially the coach of a team that needed my encouragement, training, guidance, and support to get the work done. If you embrace this first principle, it will change both how you do things and the things you do. You will be taking a major step toward implementing the other principles.

For example, let's say Tom has been promoted, and he is now in charge of a unit that processes tax information submitted by the public. Tom has been checking these forms himself for years.

Tom is afraid that if his staff makes mistakes, he will be criticized by the manager above him. He is so worried that he reviews his employees' work, looking for mistakes and constantly offering negative feedback.

If Tom had seen himself as a servant to his staff, the coach of a team, it would have changed the way that he approached his job. Rather than being a negative and critical manager, he would have taken a more positive approach to help and support staff.

As another example, let's say one of your employees seems to be dissatisfied with his job. The quality and even the quantity of his work have declined over the course of the last several weeks. He grumbles under his breath and sighs when given a new assignment. So you take him aside and reprimand him: "If your attitude and output don't change, I may be forced to take steps you will not like." Not only is this approach not likely to help, you've now added "fear" to the list of this employee's problems.

Am I right in thinking that you've been that employee at some point in your career? How would you have felt if your boss took you aside and, instead of belittling you, said, "You seem dissatisfied—how about we take a look at what's bothering you and see if we can come up with some ideas together."

When one of your employees has a problem, *you* have a problem. Solving that employee's problem goes a long way toward solving yours.

This principle also applies to higher-level managers. I have known managers who thought their job was to primarily save money. I expect managers to be concerned about costs. But as a servant leader, you should be thinking about what you can do to support your staff. Support might include things like new training, equipment, and so on. In the long run, these kinds of support can help the organization. If your employees succeed, then you succeed.

As I expand on my views, you may begin to be nervous about the risks you are taking. I am not sure that everyone has the courage and strength to manage in this manner. Using this approach, you will no longer seek to primarily criticize, blame, and look down on staff as a means to an end. Rather, you will be a positive, strong, goals-oriented coach who values your employees as coworkers and people.

Principle 2

Life Is More Important than Work

Take a real interest in your employees and try to keep their best interests in mind. Be willing to sacrifice in the short term.

I have told potential employees during interviews (and then reiterated my belief to existing employees) that our personal lives—things such as our health, families, and friends—are more important than work. I hoped that this would impress on them that I really cared about them not just as workers but also as people who have important lives outside of work. However, I also said that when we were working, we owed it to our employer to take our work seriously, work hard, and try to do the best we could.

I believe this attitude was demonstrated in my day-to-day behavior. We must be true to our words.

If someone had a family problem, sick issues, and so on, and he needed to leave, I encouraged him to go and not worry about the work. I believe the manager's job in this situation is to support the employee and to determine if the work can wait or, if not, to obtain the assistance of another staff member to do the work—or even to accept that as the manager, you may need to do the work yourself.

In practice, I found that by following my principles, my staff were quite willing to assist me to get the work done.

SOME EXAMPLES ILLUSTRATING THAT LIFE IS MORE IMPORTANT THAN WORK

I knew a woman who worked in the public sector. I will call her Jane. She was a good employee. She had dealt with breast cancer not too long ago. She had undergone radiation and chemotherapy.

A coworker who sat nearby was also recently diagnosed with breast cancer. I will call her Lois. When Jane arrived in the morning, Lois would walk over to Jane's desk and talk about what she was going through.

One morning, Jane was called into the manager's office. In an accusatory tone of voice, the manager told her that she had been seen talking with Lois in the mornings when she and Lois should each have been at her own desk working.

There are a lot of things wrong here. First is the lack of sensitivity to life issues and the accusatory tone rather than a let's-work-together attitude. Instead I would have compassion on Lois. I would talk with Lois and express my concern for her and would ask if there was anything that I could do. I would tell her that if she needed to take time off, then I would make every effort to allow her the time she needed. I would also thank her for coming to work under these circumstances.

If I considered the discussions at the desk a significant problem, I would tell Lois about the complaint. I would say to Lois that we certainly don't want to deal with complaints, especially when there is so much she is dealing with. I would suggest to avoid problems, maybe she could try shortening the time standing at Jane's desk. Perhaps they could talk on breaks or for short periods during the day.

A woman whom I will call Mary told me this very different story about a manager she thought was great. In order to receive a pay raise, Mary had to receive a performance evaluation. Unfortunately, Mary was out on sick leave. The manager actually took the time to go to Mary's home to complete the evaluation so Mary would get her raise. That's a great example of a servant manager.

I once heard an interview with the coach and key players of an NBA championship team. The coach and players talked about the teamwork that won them the championship. Teamwork included more than just how they functioned on the basketball court. They expressed how important it was that they had the support of other players and the coach, who agreed to make their personal lives, especially their families, a priority.

Even if I was providing corrective help, I kept in mind that I wanted what was best for the employee. My discussion with the employee was not just because I needed to address a problem. I really wanted to help the employee so she could do a better job and improve her career opportunities—and improve her relationship with others. This employee, like every employee, was important, and I tried to affirm that with my actions and attitude.

Principle 3

Always Try to Be Positive

This principle was so effective that I became pretty extreme in following it. I think that you should do almost anything to avoid saying negative things to your staff. Try to present everything in a positive framework. I found this to be so helpful that I would advise doing anything you can to avoid saying negative things.

BE APPRECIATIVE AND THANK PEOPLE

Generally I tried not to just give orders to people. If I needed something done, I would say something like this: "I need someone who can prepare an advertisement for this project. I would appreciate it if you could do that for me." I truly appreciated the efforts people made. I would then thank them for their help.

Even if a few employees were not particularly motivated, I tried to thank them whenever I could. Try to treat employees in a positive manner. Respect them, and treat them equally.

HOW I KEPT A POSITIVE VIEW OF MY STAFF

In order to be as positive as possible in myself, I found it helpful to try to maintain a positive view of employees. This can be difficult. Sometimes we need to resist the urge to view them as lazy and careless about their work. So here are a few insights that I found to be true and that may help you think in a positive way.

Generally, people feel bad about their mistakes. Most employees are trying to do a good job, at least from their point of view.

I think most employees want to do a good job, and most believe they are working hard. To some employees, working six hours is a full day's work. Yes, they think that they're really working hard. I learned to accept this. This perspective helped me manage these employees positively. My job was to help them be as productive as they could be. That was enough.

When I oversaw the development of an electronic consultant-selection process, I became an expert in the system and how to use it. When it was implemented, I could see that I could do the work much faster than the analysts whom I managed. I was also a very hard worker. This could have made me feel negative about my staff.

I came to believe that a skilled, highly motivated manager should not expect her staff to be as efficient and motivated as she is. Some might be, and that may be a good goal, but it is often unrealistic.

I know this goes counter to what many people believe. But I have to say that people are not all equal in skill and performance, and they are not all capable of the same work. You need to adjust your expectations for some employees.

So the manager's job is to work with the employees to help them be the best that they can be. I learned to view those I managed in a positive way.

HOW TO DEAL WITH MISTAKES BY EMPLOYEES

Especially important is dealing with employee mistakes in a positive way. When I interview someone for a job, I tell her that I understand that anyone trying to do the job will take risks and make mistakes. I tell her if there's a problem, we will first work together to fix the problem, and then we will try to learn from our mistakes and move on. I have no intention of wasting time or emotional energy in trying to blame.

I've found that employees often feel a need to protect themselves as a result of their mistakes. They have experienced managers who always wanted to blame someone if a mistake was made.

When I would sit down with employees and their supervisors, some employees would immediately try to defend themselves. It took a while for these employees to accept the fact that I meant what I said. I was not out to punish them but rather to help them.

When I say we try to learn from mistakes, I mean myself as well as my staff. When dealing with an apparent employee mistake, stop and think about whether there were some procedures that the employee might have misinterpreted or been unaware of. As managers, we should ask ourselves if there was a lack of training, or if we failed to write clear procedures for our employees. If so, those mistakes might be on our heads. We need to take responsibility.

It is important not to demean employees with harsh criticism. It is better to work together and learn together—to work as a team.

I recall an incident when an employee had stepped outside for a few minutes to smoke a cigarette. Another manager thought that we should discipline the employee. Now, this was a valuable, productive employee. Formally disciplining him would be a very negative event and against my principle of avoiding saying negative things to staff.

If I felt I had to say something, it would probably be something like this: "Another manager saw you taking a short break to smoke. You are a good employee, and I would not want to see you get in trouble, so be careful." At least this type of statement is positive and shows concern for the individual.

Here's another example. I had a thermostat near my desk. One employee asked me if she could make it cooler, and another wanted to make it warmer. I told each person I felt fine and that I was agreeable either way. Then I realized that was a negative in either direction. So we had the maintenance staff come and look at the area and to make adjustments if they could. The staff spoke with them, and in the end, both employees were satisfied.

I once heard about another office where they were planning an office party at lunchtime. The manager of the office insisted on being deeply involved. My first reaction was to wonder why a manager would want to put himself in that position. Didn't he have enough to do? And look at the potential for conflict!

The way I saw it, first the manager was going to be diverted from more important work. He certainly could let others plan the party. There are usually people who want to plan parties. Let them.

There was also a good chance that somebody wouldn't like some aspect of the planning, such as the choice of foods or beverages. People can get really upset about even minor things that affect them. Then the manager gets dragged—unnecessarily—into a negative situation.

A better approach would have been for the manager to follow my advice—always try to stay positive. A positive, hands-off manager can just attend the party and praise the planners.

Principle 4

Want What Is Best for Employees

I believe that which is best for the employee is best for the organization. If you manage the appliance section of a store, the organization is more than your section—it is the store or possibly a group of related stores. This means that you may even act in a way that seems contrary to your immediate needs to further the growth of an employee and to contribute to the organization as a whole.

Often a manager does not support employee development and growth for selfish reasons. The manager does not want to lose good employees, so she may be opposed to efforts by such employees to obtain graduate degrees or to pursue training not directly related to their present jobs—or even to their accepting promotions into different units.

However, if you want what is best for your employees, this will help create a willingness in employees to make sacrifices to help accomplish the organization's goals. I recall one of my managers saying to me that my staff would do anything for me. This was certainly partly a result of my wanting what is best for the employees.

SOME EXAMPLES OF WANTING WHAT IS BEST FOR EMPLOYEES

I tried my best to promote the professional growth of my staff to help them in their careers. I encouraged my staff to attend training.

Whenever possible, I would approve requests by employees for additional training, even if the training was not directly related to the work they were currently performing. This helps employees grow. It builds their allegiance to you, enhances your mutual relationship, and builds morale.

Frequently, more than one principle is applicable to a situation. In this example, the actions I took were consistent with the principles of always trying to be positive and remembering that life is more important than work.

If one of my staff had the opportunity to move to a different position within the organization, I tried to make this as easy as possible. I did not ask the employee to stay longer to complete some work or to ease a transition. Instead, I let such employees go as quickly and easily as possible so that they could become more motivated employees for the organization as a whole.

I once had an employee who did a good job but really wanted to be a writer. I offered to look for opportunities for him elsewhere in the organization where he might prefer to work. You see, as a servant manager, I weighed the benefits to the employee and the organization, and I was willing to let him go.

Sure, I might lose a good employee, but the organization gains a more dedicated employee, and I gain another team player if I ever need that person's help. In reality, it would be a win for everyone.

If you have trouble letting people go, remember this. If someone quits, you have to manage that situation. I treated employees who wanted to leave as if they had quit, and I let them go.

I never liked forcing people to work overtime or limiting vacations. I felt that decisions like these should be carefully weighed against positive actions that might result in more productive employees. How can you expect people to sacrifice for you if you are hurting them in their personal lives? (Naturally, this would not apply if such requests broke the terms of employment explained to the employees when they were hired.)

I said earlier that you need to do what you say. If you say that people's personal lives are more important than work, then you should act accordingly.

Principle 5

Listen to Your Staff

Whenever you consider implementing an idea, always involve your staff before moving ahead. They can identify issues that you don't see because they do the work. If your job is to help them, then you should certainly ask for their advice on something that will affect their work.

In a broader view, as a manager, I developed procedures that affected not just the staff who reported to me but many other members of the organization. It was important to involve these coworkers in the process also. This group could include managers to whom I reported, managers in other units, and so on. From my perspective, I viewed them all as team members.

Your staff can be an important source of ideas regarding changes and improvements to the work they do. They can also help you avoid mistakes. Listen to them.

Principle 6

Respect All Employees and Treat Them Equally

This means that you should value the opinions of each worker and the contributions he or she makes to the organization, regardless of your feelings about that employee personally. Treat all of your employees with respect.

For example, I once had an employee who constantly complained about other employees. I will call her Joanne. It seemed that Joanne was always looking for something negative to bring to management's attention. She felt that she worked very hard while her coworkers did not.

I would prefer that people focus on their own work rather than looking at other people. However, when Joanne complained to her supervisor because she felt that she was doing more work than others, I met with her and her supervisor to listen to the complaint.

At the meeting, I agreed to look into this matter further. My supervisor and I did an analysis of each employee's workload that showed the work was fairly distributed. I got back to Joanne, and she was satisfied.

Regardless of how you feel about an employee, treat him with respect and listen to his opinions and complaints.

Principle 7

Always Make Time for Your Staff

When your employees come to you with issues, remember that to them, these issues must be very important. Always try to give an employee the time needed to discuss a pressing issue.

Don't say you have something more important to do. If you are willing to stop what you are doing and pay attention, it demonstrates that you walk the talk. You are there for your employees, ready to help them get their jobs done. It demonstrates that they are important to you.

I learned that I needed to give up time in order to do what I said. I would give up a break, shorten my lunch, or work after hours to give employees time when they needed it.

I developed the habit of reading all my e-mails before I came back to the office following a vacation. Rather than feeling pressured to catch up on these on my first morning back, I was able to walk in and give the supervisors and staff the attention they needed. I could calmly deal with their pressing issues. One of my staff commented that she was amazed I could do this.

Now, I have heard it said employees should be told that when they come to you with problems, they should bring proposed solutions. That's ridiculous. If they knew how to solve the problem, they would not come to you.

It is frustrating for an employee to come to you for help and instead be asked for a solution to her problem. Now, instead of solving anything, you have made the situation worse.

However, when you give your employees the guidance they need to solve their problems, try to also show them the thought processes that you used to address the issues. Understanding how you solved the problem will help them to think through future situations on their own. Always look for opportunities to help employees grow.

This approach is in opposition to those who believe that people are lazy and will come to you in order to avoid thinking for themselves. Well, I suggest this is a better way.

Principle 8

Encourage Employees to Bring Forth New Ideas

You want to promote an atmosphere that encourages people to think about improving the business. I felt employees needed to be told that when they took chances, I would support them. This meant that when something went wrong, it was my job to help resolve the situation.

Whenever employees put forth new ideas, make every effort to see if those ideas can work. At the least, let your employees know that you are seriously considering their ideas and thank them. This can be a great reward for employees.

This is also great for the organization, for not only does it bring forth better ways of doing things, but it also helps employees feel like a part of the team.

Principle 9

Promote Teamwork and Organizational Goals

It is important that managers look for opportunities to encourage teamwork, support other members of the organization, and promote organizational goals. Encourage your staff to work together and to support each other and others in the organization.

EXAMPLES OF PROMOTING TEAMWORK AND ORGANIZATIONAL GOALS

In my work with any regional office (which utilizes the consultants that NYSDOT selects), I viewed us as part of a team. Often main-office staff, who are frequently experts in the details of what they do, felt the other staff were not cooperative, and they found the regional staff difficult to deal with.

My attitude was that I knew the details of my work, and it was my job to help the regional staff navigate a process that they did not fully understand and should not be expected to fully understand.

So when I dealt with my staff, I tried to encourage this view. As managers, if we adopt this view, this means that we may go out of our way and beyond our normal responsibilities to help those who need it.

When you see yourself as part of a team, then if the team succeeds, you succeed. That will hopefully make you willing to do more than just the minimum. You want to help the organization succeed. So be a team builder.

Principle 10

Empower Employees by Thoroughly Training Them

Training in this context does not just mean the formal training that employees may receive. Training also can occur when managers talk with staff in the normal course of work or when managers issue written procedures on the work.

Before I discuss training in detail, I would like to give one example of why training can be rewarding to employees.

I found that people wanted to know how to do their jobs. They wanted to look competent and feel confident. People did not like ambiguity in their work. In other words, people wanted to know how to proceed in a given situation as much as possible.

People especially dislike others seeing their mistakes; they do not like to be embarrassed. I had a number of staff members tell me that they hated publishing an advertisement on a public site and then having to revise it. This made them feel as if others would think they didn't know how to do their jobs.

So you can see why training can be positive and rewarding to employees. Here are some examples of training in this broader context.

Whenever I had the opportunity, I would explain my thought processes on a given situation. In this way, employees were learning how to work through issues on their own. To me, this was ongoing training, helping employees think for themselves.

I also tried to transfer my knowledge to my staff whenever the opportunity arose. I explained the basis for the rules we followed to give employees a deeper understanding of why and how we did things as we did. In essence, I tried my best to equip them so that I would not be needed as much.

It is extremely important to put everything you can in writing, as this helps people know how to do their work. Update these written instructions for clarity whenever necessary. If someone did not understand something, assume it was not that person's fault but yours.

If this means you spend a lot of time—at least at first—helping your employees get their jobs done, well, that is your job. Make time for it.

I've heard some managers or supervisors say that procedures cannot ever be fully complete because there are too many situations to cover. I think that is silly. If that's true, then nobody can do the job. Somebody has the answers. Put them in writing. Empower your staff.

Also, I believe most employee failures are due to inadequate training or poor supervision by managers. Managers must be clear what they expect from employees, and they must see that their employees are trained adequately.

During my last stint in management, I conducted a weekly training session for my staff. Each session was essentially a module of a process. In these training sessions, I gave the staff handouts that they could use for future reference. At these sessions, I also worked to explain why we did what we did. For example, I discussed the laws and regulations and policies and procedures that governed our work. Then I would discuss the process step by step. In this way, I was trying to transfer knowledge to them.

Principle 11

About Performance Evaluations

Personally, I never enjoyed being on the receiving end of performance evaluations. I feel that they are almost always a negative event.

When I had to prepare performance evaluations of my staff, I followed the guidance I received, and I always tried to make some good observations and then discuss opportunities for improvement. But generally, people still disliked being judged and being told where I thought they needed to improve.

This seems to be especially true of the best-performing staff. They work the hardest and are most productive. Therefore it is even more likely that such evaluations will have a negative impact.

If you are a servant manager who is truly concerned about your employees, you want what is best for them. You want to be positive and reward them, and you want to hear their ideas. Unfortunately, the performance evaluation can work against all these principles.

I'd always heard it suggested that you should start evaluations with something positive and then bring up things that needed improvement. I found that it did not help to preface negative comments with something positive. I think instead you should have an ongoing relationship with your staff. You should be thanking your staff personally and regularly for the work they are doing.

If you're coaching a team, you interact with them all the time. And if the team has problems, you talk with them and offer support and help as needed.

If you are developing an atmosphere of trust, your employees will come to you for help. You are training them. Based on your regular interactions with staff, they should really know how they're doing without a formal performance evaluation.

Maybe the performance evaluation should be replaced by a meeting to discuss employee concerns, needs, and suggestions. This is a servant manager's perspective.

Follow the principle of trying to be positive. You can offer employees opportunities to attend training, you can conduct one-to-one sit-downs to help them, or you can offer to have someone else review their work privately as a learning tool. You can tell them your goal is to help them be the best employees that they can be and to help them in their careers with the organization.

I had a situation where a new employee was working with a computer program. Her supervisor and another worker noticed a number of errors in the data that had been entered. The staff who worked with the new employee was upset about the mistakes that were being made.

I offered to meet with all of them together to address the issue. Rather than make it a meeting at which the new employee was criticized, I tried to make it a meeting that gave the new employee the tools she needed to do the work correctly. And that is what we did. The staff came up with ideas at the meeting that eliminated the mistakes.

If you must do a formal performance evaluation, follow my principles to make it as helpful and positive as you can.

Principle 12

Continually Look at the Process for Opportunities to Simplify

I continually questioned *why* things were done and *how* things were done. This process of continuous improvement is another thing you can do to help the organization and people succeed.

In a bureaucracy, I found that there were continual pressures that seemed to push toward making work more complex. This occurred because of regulations and laws, as well as internal pressures. Attorneys, in their quest to protect the agency, often added complexity to various processes.

Staff members might want to expand the checking they do. Some will fear simplification because they think it threatens their job security. I have heard people say, "If we simplify this, then they might not need someone at my level any more."

AN EXAMPLE OF HOW TO CONTINUALLY EXAMINE THE PROCESS FOR OPPORTUNITIES TO SIMPLIFY

Once, we were reviewing consultant proposals. We often got thirty or forty proposals in response to an advertisement for consultant services. The procedure up to this point required a contract specialist to review certain information in every proposal that was submitted. If the employee found errors, he would correct the proposal.

This time, we decided to only check the winning proposal and to remove an applying consultant from consideration if he or she had provided incorrect information. This made the consultants accountable for the accuracy of their proposals. It saved the contract specialists a lot of work.

DEALING WITH CHANGE

Change can be frightening to people, and it takes work to learn a new way to do things. Often employees have come to believe that the way they are operating is the best way, and they take pride and security in that. Anything that challenges this is disconcerting to them.

Therefore they and you need time to digest any change and implement it. This requires patience, as you need to help them get on board.

I think we need to manage the process of change. Help people see the benefits. Provide training. Be positive and patient. Thank them and support them.

Change, if done well, can be a lot of work for the manager. You need to recognize the many things that you need to do and make time for them. I rewrote numerous procedures to incorporate current changes that had been implemented. This is how you support your staff and help them. You succeed as they succeed.

Principle 13

Be Patient, Thick Skinned, and Long Suffering

Demonstrate true concern for each employee, and be unbelievably patient when a person is slow to learn or more difficult to bring along. At my staff meetings, I would discuss issues at length with individuals who did not agree with my direction. I allowed as much time as I could to listen to them, trying to come to a common agreement.

I had in mind a few principles in operating this way. I wanted to bring everyone along in a positive way. I was sacrificing some time in being very patient, sure, but that demonstrated to all my staff, including the dissenting individuals, that I was willing to listen to them, that I respected them, and that I treated them equally. It also encouraged us to be united as a team.

If we could not reach an agreement, I still stayed committed to my goals. I would say, "We need to move on to other matters, so for now, we will proceed as I directed. I will speak privately with anyone who would like to discuss this further."

I had one of my supervisors once ask me, "How can you be so patient?" Well, my employees and the potential long-term benefits were worth my patience.

Of course, expect those who disagree with you to bring up the subject again—especially if you had to leave it unresolved at any point. Don't become irate. Be patient. Always remember that you as a leader, mentor, and teacher have the field, so to speak. But use this privilege carefully.

Quite frequently at staff meetings, I would commit to changing a procedure for some action or other. I always encouraged people to remind me at the next staff meeting of anything that I should have done that I said I would. I always remembered that I was there to help them to get their jobs done.

You might be surprised how much good can come out of a situation, even though you may not see the results immediately. When you invest money, sometimes the profits come as compound interest. The profit seems small at first, but over time, compound interest grows into a large return.

Principle 14

Help Your Managers Succeed

As a servant manager, you should be very concerned about helping your own managers succeed. This is just a reminder that they also need you to succeed.

Regardless of where you work, managers should focus on helping the managers above them. These are a few of the things I did to serve my managers. You have to determine which things you should emphasize in your workplace.

EXAMPLES OF HOW TO HELP YOUR MANAGERS SUCCEED

I tried to protect my managers from surprise problems. I felt it was my job to make them aware of problems before they were contacted by other people.

When they requested an alternative course of action, I thought it was important to think broadly and creatively.

Since I was closer to the details of the work, I was aware of legal constraints or policies that they might not have always known about. It was my job to point these out along with the alternatives so they could make informed decisions.

I tried to think deeply about the implications of certain actions we were considering. It is possible to solve one problem but, in so doing, create unintended consequences that become other problems.

I was careful to follow up on directions from them. When I attended meetings, even if it was with an assistant commissioner, I would summarize the results and what needed to be done, who was going to do it, and when the action should be completed. I would then normally follow up with an electronic memo. I was trying to help everyone succeed by being sure that everyone understood the results and what needed to be done.

Examples of How to Apply These Principles in Real-Life Situations

I remember two situations that I dealt with in my early years as a middle-level manager that I would have dealt with differently based on my approach today. I need to share these so you can understand the dramatic changes in my view of management and how my current approach can change a bad situation into a positive one.

SITUATION 1

One day, I arrived at work and was informed that one of my staff had gotten into an argument with a technical-support person. Let's call him Tom. Tom proceeded to disconnect his computer. Then he piled up the computer, printer, and cables in one heap and refused to use it.

Well, at that time, I went to talk with Tom, and he was quite upset. I found out that he did not want to deal with the technical-support person anymore, and he had decided to have our secretarial staff deal with his e-mails so he wouldn't need a computer.

I thought he needed to use the computer and that it was not right to have the pile of equipment there for everyone to see. I directed him to put his computer back into use as I could not see how he could do his job without it. This resulted in an uncomfortable confrontation with my employee.

Which of my current principles would change my approach? First, how could I best serve Tom in a positive way as a manager? I would need to let him calm down, and then I would meet with him privately. I would be there to help him through this.

I would characterize the discussion as one intended to help him and to help us keep the office functioning as a team. I would tell him that he was a very important and productive employee whom I appreciated.

It would be negative to order him to put the computer back in action. That could wait as long as he was getting his job done.

It would be positive to ask him if he would help me deal with this situation by meeting with me and the other employee to try to work out our differences. This would make him look like a team player and would likely make him more open to discussing differences.

SITUATION 2

I had a very productive employee whom we shall call Alice. She was not busy with project work due to a slowdown in her projects. It seemed like she was taking long breaks. I spoke with her about the time issue, and she got really upset. She felt that she did a good job and worked hard whenever it was needed.

If this happened today, I would see her as a valuable employee whom I needed to help. What could I do? Perhaps I would try to find a special assignment that was important and could result in a positive experience for her. I could solicit ideas from Alice and other staff about what we could do that would help her do her job.

Maybe she could conduct a staff training on how to keep projects moving. Or perhaps she could help write new instructions on what was required from people in her position. Maybe she might like to try performing different work or getting different experiences to help her get promoted.

It's the manager's job to find what is best for all employees and help them be productive.

As a Manager, How Am I Doing? A Brief Checklist

PRINCIPLE 1: A MANAGER SHOULD BE A SERVANT LEADER

* Am I concerned about my staff as human beings?
* Do I see myself as a coach?
* Do I encourage employees, train employees, or give guidance or other support when needed? (That is, do I seek out resources for them?)

PRINCIPLE 2: LIFE IS MORE IMPORTANT THAN WORK

* Do I make sure I stay aware of any personal situations that give me the opportunity to show concern for my employees as people, to show them that life is more important than work? What do I do to help?

PRINCIPLE 3: ALWAYS TRY TO BE POSITIVE

* Do I assume that people feel badly about their mistakes, that most employees try to do a good job, and that they believe they work hard?
* If I have to deal with mistakes made by staff, do I avoid wasting time trying to blame someone? Do I instead approach the situation cooperatively? I might say something like this: "Okay, let's work through this together. If we solve the problem and learn from this, hopefully it won't happen again."
* Do I openly express appreciation for the work my staff does?

PRINCIPLE 4: WANT WHAT IS BEST FOR EMPLOYEES

* Do I use opportunities to take action that is best for the employees, such as sending them to training sessions, even on topics that I don't feel are going to directly help them do their current jobs?

PRINCIPLE 5: LISTEN TO YOUR STAFF

* Am I involved in any activity where I can encourage the opinions and/or the involvement of my staff?

PRINCIPLE 6: RESPECT ALL EMPLOYEES AND TREAT THEM EQUALLY

* Am I careful to treat all employees equally by valuing the work that they do and listening to their suggestions and complaints?

PRINCIPLE 7: ALWAYS MAKE TIME FOR YOUR STAFF

* When employees want to speak with me, do I willingly make an effort to make time for them, even if I have to do some of their work as a result?

PRINCIPLE 8: ENCOURAGE EMPLOYEES TO BRING FORTH NEW IDEAS

* Do I encourage employees to put forth new ideas? Do I do more than just give lip service to an idea? Do I go out of my way to consider it, and if I find some way to support an idea, do I give the employee credit?

PRINCIPLE 9: PROMOTE TEAMWORK AND ORGANIZATIONAL GOALS

* How do I take actions that foster teamwork? In what ways do I purposely support my staff and offer them encouragement to support other managers? In what ways do I encourage my staff to work together as a team?

PRINCIPLE 10: EMPOWER EMPLOYEES BY THOROUGHLY TRAINING THEM

* Do I take opportunities to informally train people as we interact in our daily work?
* Do I issue verbal or written instructions to clarify expectations and procedures?
* Do I try to transfer my knowledge to my employees?

PRINCIPLE 11: ABOUT PERFORMANCE EVALUATIONS

* Do I interact with my staff, discussing and solving problems with them, helping them when they need help, and generally creating a safe relationship that allows them to come to me for help?

PRINCIPLE 12: CONTINUALLY LOOK AT THE PROCESS FOR OPPORTUNITIES TO SIMPLIFY

* Do I purposely think about simplifying processes?

PRINCIPLE 13: BE PATIENT, THICK SKINNED, AND LONG SUFFERING

* Do I lose patience with my employees, or do I show great patience when helping them to grow and become more productive?

PRINCIPLE 14: HELP YOUR MANAGERS SUCCEED

* As a servant manager, how do I help the managers above me? Do I make sure they're forewarned about any potential problems?

Conclusion

This book contains what I believe are great principles to manage by. They are not everything you need to know, but by putting them into practice, I believe you will enjoy significant benefits in your work as a manager.

About the Author

Edward Schmidt was a manager at the New York State Department of Transportation for sixteen years. While there, he oversaw the key project to create the New York State Department of Transportation's first electronic consultant-selection system. This was important because consultants designed about half of the highways and bridges to be built. He then took on the role of managing two groups involved in hiring consultants.

After receiving great feedback from other managers and employees, he decided to write this guidebook to help managers establish positive relationships and workplaces.

Schmidt has a bachelor's degree in civil engineering.

www.ingramcontent.com/pod-product-compliance
Lightning Source LLC
Chambersburg PA
CBHW070407190526
45169CB00003B/1151